Pretty Wings

Natashia Hagans

BookLeaf Publishing

Presentation by *BookLeaf Publishing*

Web: www.bookleafpub.com

E-mail: info@bookleafpub.com

ISBN: 9789357211888

First edition 2023

DEDICATION

This book is for women who have been victims of physical, emotional, sexual, psychological, and financial abuse at the hands of their abuser and for those who lost their lives to domestic violence.

ACKNOWLEDGEMENT

I wish to show mindfulness to women who are victims and survivors of domestic violence.

PREFACE

Natashia Hagans wrote the poetry book 'Pretty Wings' to explore domestic violence; so many women have suffered in silence. To let women who are still victims of abuse know that their wings are pretty, and also for those who are no longer in abusive relationships but are still struggling with the aftermath.

Straight Facts

Here are the straight facts
For the victims of domestic violence abuse
It might look like just hitting
Sad to say, that isn't so
There are six types of abuse
Physical
sexual
emotional
psychology
financial
and the last is a shocker technology

Here are the straight facts
Knowledge is powerful
Domestic violence affects one million people in America
Predominantly 85% of the people are women
it makes me think men are victims too

Here are the straight facts
Folks might think domestic violence is a loss of temper
No, the abuser is making a conscious decision to lose their cool
The temper tantrum is to control the victim through fear

Here are the straight facts

Folks might believe that drinking and drugs cause domestic violence
Let's rewind that back; it isn't a fact
It's an excuse for violent behavior
But substance abuse might increase the severity of abuse

Straight facts
The abuser tells the victim they are sorry and won't do it again
But in reality, begging for forgiveness is manipulation
The abuser rarely stops
As time goes by, the abuse gets worse

Last but not least
The victim has a personality that encourages abuse
Whatever,
There are no universal personality traits
That triggers the abuse
It is the abuser who is responsible for the abuse

The Straight facts

911

She races to the phone in horror with bruised
knuckles.
Screaming so loud
With a busted lip and black eye
She manages to dial the number 911
Blood dripping down from her lips

Dispatcher: “911 How May I help you?”
Dispatcher “Is this an emergency?”
As she looks up, the man that gives her
nightmares appears
He knocks the phone out of her hands
He growls
He boldly tells her
“Hang up the phone before I kill you right here.”

She drops the phone with a blank stare
He puts his hands around her neck
She just knew she would get away today
She looks at him dead in the face
Screaming in her mind
This relationship was a mistake

A loud banging noise at the door startled them both
He releases his hands from her neck
With a calm voice while staring at her
He states: “Who is it?”
She knew then to go upstairs to wash her face

Quickly put on some make up and stay her place

911: “Someone called 911 from this location. Is everything ok?”
He opened the door with a grin
“Yes, everything is cool.”
He looks behind him
As she walks down the stairs with a beautiful glare
She: “Yeah, babe, everything is good.”
Putting one foot in front of the other

She tells the police everything is fine and dandy
They look around and go about their business
He closes the door
She backs up
In her head, round two is coming
He calmly takes a gun out of his pocket
He points it to her forehead

The gun frightens her
So she froze

She knew to stay in position
Don’t move
He whispers to her:
“Call 911 again next time; this gun won’t make
any mistakes.”
As he smacks the gun in her face

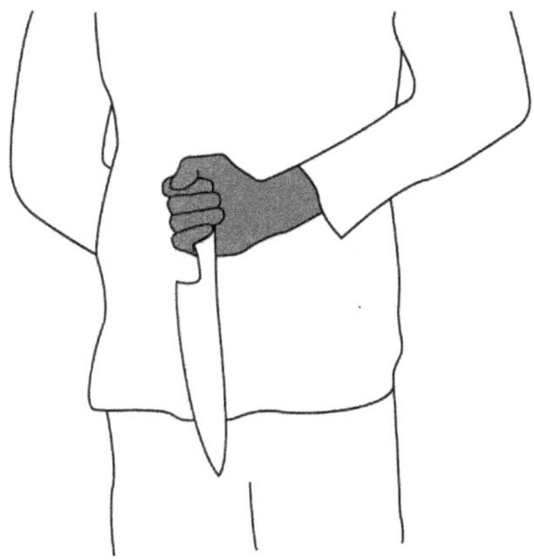

Final destination

I called the cops on you too many times
To tell them everything is just fine
To give them a celebratory smile
As I closed the door
I ran to the stairs hoping not to face rage
I ran faster and faster up those long stairs
To hear a boom
Not knowing it was me who got shot
I thought in my head,
Where could all this blood be coming from
Another boom boom from the gun you held
My breathing became slow
I fainted walking up the stairs
My head clouding out
I saw heaven near
I couldn't look back
No point in saying our goodbyes
You made sure the bullets shattered my sunset
spine
I felt relief, though, because I lived in hell
But Heaven was emerging
As I took my last breath and clasped to the
ground
I tumbled into the wall, soaked in blood
Making it to my final destination
With no hopes and despair

I know you love me though

You put your hands on me again
You verbally talked down on me in front of my friends.
It's ok.
I know you stress and had to get stuff off your chest
But I know you are the only one who loves me though

Been physically and emotionally abused since I was a child
So when we makeup, it fills the void
You buy me designer bags that makes me so happy
You gift me with the Jordan 23
So I know you love me though

I wear a lot of makeup to cover the bruises
Even really baggy clothes to hide the scars
When we fight, I get an adrenaline rush
Never had anyone paid attention to me this much
So I know you love me though

When I feel your tender touch

Or when you give me an aggressive shove
No one can take your place
Because in my eyes, you are honest and raw
You are my number one fan
You are always there
So I know you love me though

When telling me you kill me if I leave
I smile
You would do that for me
Man, that's love
I would feel silly without you
If I didn't have you, I'd be searching for the moon
I would be incomplete without you
You're my other half
Because I know you love me though

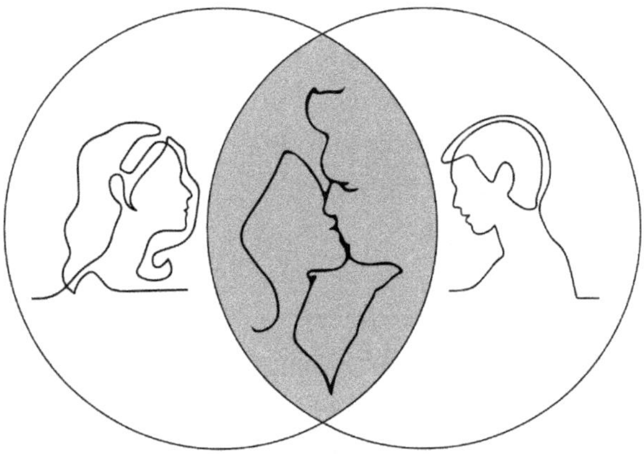

Freeze the Money

I work hard for the money
But my significant other just won't let up
Take every ounce of my cash
I don't even have a secret stash

I work hard for the money
But my partner won't let up
Make me hand over my paycheck
Every chance they get

I work hard for the money
But my dude won't let up
He takes it to the bank
He watches me as I put his name on my account

I work hard for the money
But she won't let up
I went to get some cash from the atm
She didn't leave me a dime
That I brought in

I work hard for the money
I mean, I work hard for the money
To have it snatched away
It's like slowly drowning in the ocean

Only to come to shore
And drown again

I work hard for the money
But my account is on constant freeze
Again and again
I can't seem to breathe

Black and Blue

The physical punches
are leaving me black and blue
One after the other

The mosaic of my face
It used to be pretty
But now it's stained with blows of black and
blue

As I look in the mirror to use pallets of makeup
I'm a cold-hearted artist
Trying to get rid of the black and blue

Every time I tell him to stop
The hits get harder
The blacks and blues glitters like stardom

I wonder if I should cover them up anymore
Just let it flow
These blacks and blues around my eyes

Or should I wear it
For the world to see
What he has done to my face
Printed it with black and blue

Not tonight

I know we said our vows
I love you
Til death do us part
But not tonight
I don't want to have sex with you

Can't you chill
Why are you ripping my blouse off
I know we said our vows
But not tonight
I don't want to make love to you

Hubby, why are you snatching my panties off
I know our vows
Why are you dangling your manhood in my face
I said not tonight

I turn my head to the wall
You snatched me up
I have no desire to please you today
I know our vows
Just not tonight, homeboy

As you throw me across the bed
I scream with terror
I know our vows

But I try my best to shove you off of me
I whisper not tonight

You slam in me with only your pleasure
Gyrating deep within
I cry because I know our vows
But it seems you violated me
Damn, you raped me

When you finish doing what you do
I run to the bathroom
Turn the sink on and let the water run
Wipe between my legs
To get you off of me

As I cry
I know we said our vows
But said not tonight
And you took it upon yourself
To violate me when I said not tonight

Survived

I survived things in life I wasn't ready for
The abuse started early
Around the age of thirteen
My first boyfriend forced a hickey on my neck

By the time I was 20,
I survived horrible abuse
Every boyfriend I messed with hit me
Verbally abusing me
Controlled my every move

I survived an extension cord being wrapped
around my neck
Beaten bloody and pushed into the streets
I almost lost my life that day
A car just missed me

I survived being isolated
Had no friends
I would be locked in the room for hours
Being told no man would want me

I survived being dragged by my hair
You should see the holes in the wall
It was seconds away from my face being.
smashed in

So when you see me.
Singing off tune to destiny child's song I’m a survivor
Just know I’ve survived
some horrendous things

I am not a Victim

Remembering only distraught thoughts
Flooding my mind
I reminisce on the abuse
Sometimes it is hard for others to understand
That he meant to hurt me with his hands

I felt like everyone was against me
So I numbed the pain with many shots of tequila
and pipes filled with crack
To forget those horrible days
Of being abused

Now I look at that cloud of darkness as a small
fraction of my life
I refuse to be a victim
I will hold my head high and look at the
sunshine
That color of life, imagination, and dreams

All I needed was for the sun to shine on me
Spark a revolution in my soul
To realize my true self
The way to approach the world

They say when it rains, it pours
But I do know that through rain, flowers will grow
And life will never give me a seed that I can't sow
So my dark struggle helped my wings to take flight

This journey called life is far from over
But I refused to be labeled as a victim
I have too much potential
To stay wrapped up in my past tense

My voice will echo for those who need hope
I might struggle with the flashbacks of the past
But life must go on even if you see a glimpse of my tears
I want everyone to know I'm not a victim

Silence

You tormented me
But I remained in silence
You mentally and emotionally abused me
Which at times made me go insane

The way you yelled at me
The horrible things you said
left me crushed in silence
I know you could tell

But you loved hurting me,
Your ego smiled through
When you verbally cussed me out
You always yelled at me
Telling me, I had a lot to lose

I stayed in silence
For I believed your words to be true
So I said nothing,
Wishing one day, you would stop soon.

I know I didn't deserve it,
Buy I stayed in silence.
Because I thought I'll always have to endure it,

You see, I stayed in silence
Because I felt like a caged bird
With no voice

Phone on Lock

It might sound stupid my significant other has
my phone on lock

Something so small as a smartphone

It's on lock in the bedroom
In the bathroom,

Even in restaurants.

Even while making dinner, while eating, and
after eating

It seems as if my significant other's eyes never
sleep

So I turn in my smartphones every night

It's attached to my abuser's hip

It feels like the police are monitoring me

Something so small has so much power

I can't even relax anymore.

His eyes are on my phone like hot glue

Watching my Facebook notification, email reminders, and social media accounts

And all the apps.

I have no control over my life

Because of my significant other's insecurity

My phone is on lock

It makes me so sad

Turmoil

There is a turmoil in my home,
The victim is my mother
At a young age, it frightened me
To see my mother get punched with a fist

It wasn't a normal childhood at all
Because my mother's face
Seemed to
Always stay in so many places
While I wept for her from the floor

Daddy always left trails of fingerprints
Prints that reached my soul
I tried to scrub the turmoil away,
But daddy always seemed to ruin my day

There were many witnesses,
Besides my mother's two black eyes
But they always seem to turn the other way
Claiming they couldn't see the turmoil
Oh the lies

After seeing the turmoil for so long
There were no tears ahead
A whole lot of anger
Built up instead

As I said, daddy left many clues
In my mother's face, you could see every trace of abuse
Every memory of it cause me turmoil,
Which I could never erase

The police never found my mother's tormented body,
Because she stayed around.
I didn't understand why she would stay
It made me lost inside
I couldn't understand why she didn't want to be found

There was always a weapon of choice
He used on mommy,
It was an extension of him
It was his fist
As I watch her get attacked
My heart became so grim.

The turmoil wasn't typical,
It never ended
You see, my mother is still with that man
Right at this moment
Mommy chose daddy
While I have scars
To face another day

Ride or Die

Please look at the phrase ride or die so
differently
I'm here to tell you my story

I was out with my friends one day
I had their back
I thought they definitely would have my front
Or so I thought

One night at a local club
My ride a die, and I was having a good time
Drinking shots after shots of tequila
Dancing to every club track, there was

Dude came over who I didn't really
know
I thought nothing of it because he was always
around
He offered to buy me a drink
I was hesitant, but what the heck
He seemed cool

After a couple more drinks
My head got fuzzy
Everything looked like a daze

See, one of my rides or dies
Was pissed
Because the slick guy
Was what she was digging

So she waited until I turned my head
And dropped a molly
In my red cup
It didn't take much
I suddenly felt woozy
And I fell to the ground

And everything after that became blurred
Now, as I'm an ancestor
I'm trying to get
My folks' attention
Of what happened to me

My story is a mystery
Those rides or dies
watched as he raped me from behind

I tried so hard to get away
But the cocaine in him took complete control
And he strangled me
Where my ride or die
While I'm being abused
Nowhere to be found

And now my family broke heartened
By my ride or die's bull shit story

Mirror

As you look into the mirror
The bruises
can be covered with makeup,
foundation packed on
but you can't cover the hurt;
you can't hide the wrong.

While looking in the mirror
You disguise your eyes
all black and blue,
With mac foundation and cover girl blues
But nothing can hide what that man has done to
you

As you look into the mirror
You hide the scratches
The marks
But deep down inside, you can feel his bites and
marks

As you look into the mirror
Some scars can’t be looked over
The ones invisible to the eye
The words that cut like a knife
The wounds that stayed the longest.

As you look into the mirror
Your makeup put another artist to shame
but you only wear it for a hedge of protection
Not for fame

As you look in the mirror
You want so badly to hide the pain you feel
You tremble as you look at the bites, marks, and bruises
How he threw away your heart.

As you look into the mirror
All tattered and torn,
Your self-worth all gone,
second guessing yourself,
thinking everything you do is wrong.

As you look into the mirror
You look in disbelief
At how dark and cloudy his soul could be
To torment a pretty face
You want everything just to go away

Ups and downs

For so many days, my mind has had its ups and downs
Reminding me of the abuse I had to face
Why must you come back almost every day?
It reminds me of the pain
Can it please just go away

My mind has its ups and downs again
Tears, tears flowing so fast
The abuse and scars just can't be erased
It takes a toll on my mind
Each day I think I'm going to break

My mind keeps having ups and downs
But I do remember I did escape
So please don't be so hard on me
Healing isn't a race

Innocence

My innocence looks at you through the door,
When you looked at me with them lustful eyes
I knew it was going to be a horrendous night;

Knots in my tummy started to tremble
At night my innocence tries to block out your
smoky, bitter breathe
I attempted to vomit with each kiss
Your body is foreign to mine

My innocence wants to play with doll babies
Also, wrap my hair up in curls
But as you roughly caress me
My once dreams become nightmares

This affair has been going on for too long
I was six, then
Now I'm eighteen
Living with you in despair

You see, I'm innocent
At the tender age of twelve
The ladies asked me why my butt was too big
Why is my tremendous breasts so plump
Why I'm so fast

I didn't tell them to mush I just kept on the hush

You see, I'm innocent I swear
When I ran away from home
I looked for love
In men just like you

Didn't find true love
So I stayed reckless and confused

Puppy love

This puppy love
I'm so in love with you
A love so sudden and so sweet,
You have me in glee with flowers
Then one day, you gave ma kiss with your fist
I became confused

I wondered how puppy love could be so wrong
It went wrong so fast
but I refuse to stay away
Because your smile stole my whole day
Had me dangerously in love
I was in love with Bonnie and Clyde

Puppy love blinded me
It had my legs wobbly
Every time you looked at me, my body turned
into clay
I refused to walk away.
I just stayed and prayed

This puppy love got way too deep
I started not to recognize myself
Because the blows started running deep
I could not see a single thing

How did this puppy love become a nightmare on
Elm Street
I mean, a real-life horror story
The trees and bushes started speaking to me

How did this puppy love distort us
That on a cold, snowy day
After a violent argument
I snapped and stabbed you

How did puppy love get me into jail
I silently cried out for help
Now I'm in prison, about to melt
This sweet face didn't make a mistake

How does puppy love make you feel faded
As I stand before the judge in an orange suit
Knowing my fate before the speech
Yeah, I meant to stab you
I have no remorse
As I look at you in disgust

It became Clear

It became clear
Out of the blue
I had to leave
Never go back.
I won't go back
I just can't

It became clear
When you slapped me
To run as fast as I can
Not giving you time
To find me by your naked hands

It became clear to me when I had enough
Of the physical abuse
Sexual abuse
Verbal and emotional abuse
It was damn time that I must leave

It became clear that I had to leave
Take none of my belongs
None of the memories
I had to go ghost
So you could never find me
You feel me

It became clear that I became cold-hearted
But the jabs you took on my heart
Played the part
Player
So I played chess
You ran out of checkers without your girl

It became clear that I had to leave
I knew that your heart was ice blue
Knowing that someone you once controlled
Is millions and miles away from you

It became clear that I had to leave
I was bitter,
Your ego is bruised
I didn't want to break up the happy home
By slicing you up with a knife
So I went on and left
My Dear

Secrets

Yeah, no one has to know
Yeah, no one has to know
Not my family
Not my friends
Hell not even God
Our little secret
It is between you and me

I'm too embarrassed to talk about
Because in front of everyone else, I'm tough
I'm gangsta
They definitely would not believe
The secrets between you and me

I go around town drinking the gangsta lean
To keep my mind off of things
I will fight chick over you
Slice her face up
Because I pretend to be that hard
Yes, the li'l secret is just between me and you

Every time I have a black eye
I blame it on the streets
Tell a beautiful Lie
How I got into a scuffle

Little do they no know that you are the one that's doing the shuffle

Yeah, it's a secret
I promised never to tell
That you beat my ass every day
I feel so ashamed
I'm the one to fucking blame

Blow by Blow

Thrown to the floor
Every hit hurt
I felt a blow to the nose
Being verbally raped with words
I listened to the tragic impact
I started using drugs to numb the pain
You even spat on me
The choke holds damaged me
Yeah, I felt every blow-by-blow
How can I cheer up
When I face abuse each day
It's too many blows after blows

Pretty Wings

Hold your pretty wings up high
You have been battered and bruised
Torn and confused
Face a lot of trauma
That was even too much for your mama

Hold up your pretty wings so high
You have been called stupid and worthless
And even felt ugly and misused
Been called every cuss word in the book
You are fragile and shouldn't have been abused

Hold up your pretty wings so high
That your wings touch the heavens
Find the mosaic art in you
Who you are today is enough
Believe it and let it be true

Hold your pretty wings up so high
Let them boldly fly
Unapologetic for what you have been through
Leaving trails of wisdom in you

Hold your pretty wings up so high
With each feather holding a message

Of triumph, hope, despair, resilience, and vulnerability
Hold these melodies of feathers in your bosom
Let it be

Hold your pretty wings up so high
To the sun
May it be your shelter
Stay there when you feel down
Don't flinch, and may you
Never again run or feel
As if you have to disappear

Hold your pretty wings up so high
the moon won't take away your truth
Embrace your darkness upon its shadows
Let it flourish
May you always bloom

Hold your pretty wings up so high
let your glow
Embrace all of humanity
Don't be embarrassed about your horrific story
But to help another victim find a haven
So they to can march to their story

Hold your pretty wings up so high
Embracing everything with love
Knowing your story will help someone

Without a doubt
Run their course without remorse

www.ingramcontent.com/pod-product-compliance
Lightning Source LLC
Chambersburg PA
CBHW051739130826
49812CB00033B/929
9789357211888